1 MONTH OF
FREE
READING

at

www.ForgottenBooks.com

By purchasing this book you are eligible for one month membership to ForgottenBooks.com, giving you unlimited access to our entire collection of over 700,000 titles via our web site and mobile apps.

To claim your free month visit:

www.forgottenbooks.com/free241329

ISBN 978-0-483-40436-6
PIBN 10241329

Manuals of Faith and Duty.

EDITED BY REV. J. S. CANTWELL, D.D.

A SERIES of short books in exposition of prominent teachings of the UNIVERSALIST CHURCH, and the moral and religious obligations of believers. They are prepared by writers selected for their ability to present in brief compass an instructive and helpful Manual on the subject undertaken. The volumes will be affirmative and constructive in statement, avoiding controversy, while specifically unfolding doctrines.

The MANUALS OF FAITH AND DUTY are issued at intervals of three or four months ; uniform in size, style, and price.

No. I. THE FATHERHOOD OF GOD.
By Rev. J. COLEMAN ADAMS, D.D., Chicago.

No. II. JESUS THE CHRIST.
By Rev. S. CRANE, D.D , Norwalk, O.

No. III. REVELATION.
By Rev. I. M. ATWOOD, D D., President of the Theological School, Canton, N. Y.

No. IV. CHRIST IN THE LIFE.
By Rev. WARREN S. WOODBRIDGE, Medford, Mass.

No. V. SALVATION.
By Rev. ORELLO CONE, D.D., President of Buchtel College, Akron, O.

Number VI. of the Series will be : " The Birth from Above," by Rev. Charles Follen Lee. Other volumes and writers will be announced hereafter.

PUBLISHED BY THE

UNIVERSALIST PUBLISHING HOUSE,

BOSTON, MASS.
Western Branch: 69 Dearborn Street, Chicago.

𝕸anuals of 𝕱aith and 𝕯uty.

No. V.

SALVATION.

BY

ORELLO CONE, D.D.,

PRESIDENT OF BUCHTEL COLLEGE, AKRON, O.

R THE LAW OF THE SPIRIT OF LIFE IN CHRIST JESUS HATH
MADE ME FREE FROM THE LAW OF SIN AND DEATH.

Romans viii. 2.

BOSTON:

UNIVERSALIST PUBLISHING HOUSE.

1889.

University Press:
John Wilson & Son, Cambridge.

CONTENTS.

Of those who care for religion, the multitude of us want the materialism of the Apocalypse; the few want a vague religiosity. Science, which more and more teaches us to find in the unapparent the real, will gradually serve to conquer the materialism of the popular religion. The friends of vague religiosity, on the other hand, will be more and more taught by experience that a theology, a scientific appreciation of the facts of religion, is wanted for religion; but a theology which is a true theology, not a false.

MATTHEW ARNOLD.

SALVATION.

———◆———

INTRODUCTION.

EVERY religion presupposes an unnatural, discordant relation of man to the spiritual laws of his being. Perfect, he would have no need of a religion, and would never originate one. Dependent and fallible, the sharp sense of weakness and spiritual want he cannot cast out, nor can he escape the obtrusive presence of the higher Powers. Deep mystery surrounds him, in which he can read little save the characters of law, written large and luminous. Finding himself out of harmony with the great order into which he is cast, he is filled with unrest, and sets himself to a solution of the problem of reconciliation. This consciousness of discord and the struggle with the problem how to attain harmony denote the beginning of religion, and his solution of the problem marks the degree and character of his spiritual insight.

If his thought do not rise above Nature, his religion will begin and end in a propitiation of her supposed malign forces. If he attain the apprehension of a personal benignant Power and Will superior to the natural order, originating and imposing a moral law, his religion will be a sense of dependence upon God, worship, communion, aspiration for harmony with Him, indestructible confidence and faith. The nature of his idea of God will determine his conception of salvation.

Salvation implies a bondage in certain evil conditions from which it is a deliverance. It sinks in man's thought to the level of release from temporal misfortune, social or political calamity, sorrow, physical pain or discomfort, or rises into the realm of purely spiritual relations, according to the note of his interpretation of the Supreme Being. Accordingly, its doctrine of salvation reveals the inmost character of a religion. It is its vital part. Herein does religion affect man most powerfully, because herein it immediately touches his life. His conduct sinks to a lower or rises to a higher point according as, through his conception of salvation, he apprehends his relation to God. Whether in his worship he shall grovel in rites, ceremonies, and bloody offerings, in propitiation and atonement, to reconcile an offended and changeable Deity, or in spirit and truth rise into communion with Him who is a Spirit, is largely determined by his ideas regarding this central point in religion.

As a *moral* being, capable of conceiving an ideal development and endowed with a passion for its attainment, man cannot but be restless under the bondage of his lower impulses, and struggle with an energy proportional to his ethical enlightenment for deliverance, or salvation, from the degradation into which they bring him. The most intensely interesting and pathetic part of the story of his life is the record of this struggle. As a *spiritual* being, believing in God as a moral Governor and Father, the sense of this discord between his higher and lower nature is sharpened to its acutest note in the consciousness of sin. In the Biblical conception of man this latter relation is brought into prominence with great pathos and power. Very significant, too, it is that on the first page of the Bible, in the legend of the Fall, is sounded a joyful note of deliverance in the announcement that the seed of the woman, the essential man, — man realizing the Divine plan, — shall be victorious in the contest with the seed of the serpent, the rude and brutal forces of his nature. The bitterness of this conflict is manifested in the long and all but hopeless struggle of the Prophets with the obduracy of their people, gives a tone of sadness and despondency to many a Biblical writing, and finds intensest expression in the sharp cry of despair and pain wrung from the soul of the great Apostle to the Gentiles.

I. — Salvation in the Old Testament.

If the sense of bondage to sin is profound in the human soul, not less so is that of the urgency of deliverance from this condition. No more sagacious interpretation of human nature in this relation has been made by any of the great teachers of men than is furnished in the works of the conspicuous writers of the Old Testament. So obvious is this to every careful and unbiassed student of these writings, that one hazards nothing in saying that the religion of the Old Testament is pre-eminent among the religions of antiquity for the distinctness and energy of its conception of salvation. Whatever may be thought of the remedy which it proposes for sin, however limited its spiritual horizon may be deemed, its vigorous accentuation of the dreadful fact of sin and of the urgeney of deliverance from the bondage of the violated law is indisputable.

The writers of the Old Testament set forth no philosophy of sin, either regarding its origin or nature, and do not attempt a solution of the problems which it has presented to the reflection of later ages. With the exception of the author of the book of Job, they do not enter with serious purpose upon metaphysical inquiries. One of the two documents which eriticism traces in the Pentateuch (the Elohistic) does, indeed, give a mythical account of the Fall of man and of the entrance of sin into the world, assuming the human race to have begun its existence in a state of childlike innocence and ignorance of good and evil. But the Jehovist narrator knows nothing of all this, and there are no decided marks of its influence in the later writers. The doctrine of Original Sin, as it has unhappily been set forth in Christian theology, finds no support in the canonical books of the Old Testament. The natural weakness

and tendency to sin in man are recognized, —
that the imagination of his heart is evil; that
he was shapen in iniquity and conceived in sin;
that he dwells in a house of clay, and has his
foundation in the dust,[1] etc. It is thus taught
that man has in a certain sense inherited sin,
that is, has received by heredity the germ of its
development, and is, accordingly, to a degree
excusable; that God has not willed it, but only
set the possibility of it in man, whom He has
created with the power of self-determination
and of overcoming in the struggle with evil
passions.

The Hebrew conception of sin finds its ex-
planation only in connection with the theocratic idea. From this it receives its predominant
tone, although there is not a little teaching
which proceeds upon general ethical and spiritual principles. The law, the ceremonial pre-
scriptions, the entire cultus are enjoined upon
the people as expressing the will of Jehovah,
the theocratic head of the nation; and the greatest importance could not but be attached to all
acts and observances by which a true citizen of
the theocracy was distinguished from the rest

---

[1] Genesis viii. 21; Psalm li. 7; Job iv. 17.

of mankind. Hence the externality which characterized all expression of religion, and the degenerate formalism which stifled worship. How deep-seated this perversion was, appears in the vehement denunciations of the ceremonial observances by the Prophets, who stand forth, one might almost dare to say, as the preachers of a new morality and religion, and teach that only he who is of a contrite spirit and trembleth at the word of God shall find favor in His sight. Yet are not the Prophets themselves outdone in the denunciation of theocratic sins, or offences against Jehovah as the Ruler of the nation, who resents as injuries to Himself all acts prejudicial to its welfare.

The immediate *personal* relation of sin to Jehovah is strongly set forth in the Hebrew theology and theodicy. Jehovah is represented as having His people in charge, as having entered into a covenant with them and earnestly seeking their welfare. On His part the covenant is sacredly kept, for He is the Righteous One. Through the teachers and Prophets whom He has commissioned, His will has been made known and strictly enjoined. But the people are unrighteous, breakers of the covenant, idol-

aters. Their violation of the law is characterized as sedition, revolt, apostasy. It is an
arrant wrong, a foolish wickedness, an aimless
and unsubstantial proceeding, since it is di-
rected against the All-Powerful, who will smite
His enemies with confusion and overthrow.
Enemies of God, indeed, are they who break
His covenant and disobey His law, and " He will
wound their head and hairy scalp." The an-
thropopathism of the Hebrew writers, of which
a considerable residuum is left after due allow-
ance has been made for Oriental modes of expression, has colored their idea of sin as related
to the Deity, and perhaps led them to give ex-
cessive prominence to this side of it. The
wrath of God against His " enemies," however
these writers may have conceived it, and the
swift overthrow which awaits them, are expressions so often recurring that they can hardly
be regarded as merely poetic ornaments of
speech. Rather, such words convey what to
those who so constantly use them was a terrible
reality.

The phase of sin in which it is immediately
related to man — its human side — is likewise
set forth in the Old Testament with thorough

earnestness and in a tone of energetic warning. The swift and certain consequences of disobedience are proclaimed; mischief and destruction pursue the transgressor, and no human acumen, no joining of hand in hand, can avert the doom. Are not the eyes of the Lord in every place? The wings of the morning cannot bear one where He is not in His protecting or avenging power.

The consequences of sin, and therefore the nature of salvation, are, however, more definitely determined from the point of view of the theocracy. Sin, as ordinarily treated in the Old Testament, being a theocratic offence, receives in reference to its effects a theocratic interpretation. Now the theocracy, being regarded from the " particularistic " point of view as a temporal order of things, must find its completion in the world. Accordingly, the Hebrew view of sin does not include a retribution future to the present life. In the story of the Fall, death is announced as the penalty of disobedience. But this doctrine appears to have exerted no influence upon Hebrew theology. Indeed, the account is not, on the surface at least, consistent with itself; for in Genesis iii. 19, man is spoken of as naturally mortal, and in verse 22 it is implied that the only way to prevent his acquiring immortality is to cut off his approach to the tree of life. Hence death cannot be regarded, according to the legend itself, as the consequence of disobedience, unless indirectly, through exclusion from the garden where man might have eaten of the unforbidden tree of life.

The popular Hebrew doctrine of the relation of death to sin is not, however, without close relation to this ancient tradition thus interpreted. For while length of days and temporal prosperity are regarded as the sure reward of the righteous, it is taught that the expectation of the wicked shall perish, that their days shall be shortened, — like sheep are they laid in the grave.[1] On the other hand, long life is promised as the reward of obedience to the law of God; and life and good, death and evil, are set over against each other in the solemn summary of the divine order of the theocracy.[2] Probably no stronger and intenser expressions of the temporal disaster which a wicked life may cause are found in any literature than the Biblical

---

[1] Proverbs x. 25, 27; Psalm xlix.
[2] Exodus xx. 12; Deuteronomy xxx. 15–20.

writers employ. Their insight is in this regard remarkably clear. They are seers to whom the wisdom of ages and the lessons of human experience stand forth clearly defined in their naked reality. In how fine a contrast are the ways of the righteous and of the evil doer set in these words: " The path of the just is as the shining light, that shineth more and more unto the perfect day ; " but " the way of the wicked is as darkness : they know not at what they stumble." How terrible the picture of the wicked man, whose spiritual vision is dimmed, going down into ever-increasing darkness, and at last losing moral discernment, so that he does not know at what he stumbles !

The fact, however, that in actual life the wicked often appear prosperous, and the righteous suffer affliction, presented to the Hebrew a problem which he could not solve by postponing the adjustment to a future life, because of the temporal limitation of his view. He comforted himself as best he could with the reflection that the death of the wicked must be as dreadful as that of the righteous was beautiful and full of peace. In despair of any solution of this problem, some of the less devout and perhaps less profound

adopted the point of view of pessimistic indiffer-
entism, which found expression in the epicurean
motto, " Let us eat and drink, for to-morrow
we die." The pious, however, cherished such
slender consolation as they could find in their
temporal hopes. The happiness of the wicked
endures, they reasoned, only for a day; speedily
are they hurried off the scene of existence : but
the righteous are delivered from the peril of
death, and at least may enjoy a long life and a
peaceful demise. In the admonitions of the
writer of Proverbs, in the exhortations of the
Prophets, and in the warning and exulting
strains of the Psalmists, a utilitarian practical
wisdom attains a most energetic expression.

The Hebrew conception of salvation was determined by that of sin and its consequences, as
held under the law and by the Prophets. Salvation, so far as it was legally and ethically
regarded, was simply a bondage to the law.
Deliverance, indeed, it was from the bondage
which the broken law imposed in the form of
penalty ; but under the intolerable burden of
ceremonial and a tedious cultus, he still remained
who had performed the rites and offered the
atoning sacrifice. Jehovah, through the law,

was the Saviour who, by severe discipline, force, and penalty, restrains the evil passions of men. He is conceived as the Supreme Lawgiver and Executive, a being of unapproachable majesty, revealing Himself in the terrific forces of Nature, — in thunder, lightning, earthquake. A free, joyous, and peaceful development, a hopeful striving to attain an ideal spiritual life, a serene abiding in love and communion with God as Father, were necessarily impossible from this theological point of view. Salvation is a negation, a release from fear and pain, rather than an impulse to a fresh and positive ethical striving. No one who has understood the real nature of the Hebrew legalism will think Paul's arraignment of it too strong. There is a note of melancholy, a sense of bondage and weariness in that vast system of formalism and severity, which are in strong contrast with the joyful consciousness of liberty, expressed by no one with more force and fervor than by this same Paul. Not wholly wanting, indeed, to the Hebrew religious poetry are the cheerful tone of mind and the exhortation to rejoice in the Lord. But how often does the spirit in which the rejoicing is called for throw over it a veil of sad-

ness! — " Let the people tremble ; " " a fire go-
eth before Him and burneth up His enemies."

As a means of counteracting or breaking the
relentless force of the law and furnishing deliverance, or salvation, from its curse, sacrifices
held a prominent place in Hebrew legalism. In
the vast number of cases in which the law was
violated through ignorance, weakness of the
flesh, or error, provision was made to atone for
the fault, to make restitution, by the offering of
sacrifices to avert the withdrawing of the Divine
favor and the retributive consequences of the
offence. It is not to the present purpose to
enter into a minute account of the sacrificial
prescripts. Suffice it to remark that the com-
parative history of religions shows the high antiquity and wide prevalence of propitiatory
offerings to the gods. The institution of sacrifices was not of Mosaic origin, nor does the
elaborate form of the ceremonial as it is laid
down in the Pentateuch date from an earlier
period than the age of Solomon. The religious
feeling out of which the sacrificial system and
ceremonial sprang, was that the Divine favor
could be secured by the offering of some valu-
able possession. The burnt-offering was an

expression of reverence towards God, of devotion to Him, and willingness for His service. The thank-offering was a return for a benefit received. The sin-offering expressed an acknowledgment of the disturbance through transgression of the peaceful relation with the Deity, and was offered with a view to reconciliation, to annulment of the sin in the sense that its penal consequences should not follow if the sacrifice were graciously received. Symbolical, perhaps, in a general sense, these sacrifices were. But there can be little doubt that the sin-offering was regarded as substitutional, or at least as furnishing satisfaction for the offence on account of which it was made. " The life of the flesh," which " is in the blood," " is given upon the altar to make an atonement for the life " of the transgressor, forfeited by the sin.[1] The analogy of other ancient religions is not without significance in relation to the interpretation of this sacrificial rite. Precisely in this idea of the importance in itself of the external side of the sacrifice lay the imperfection and the peril of the

[1] Leviticus xvii. 11. This view is philologically established by the fact that the Hebrew word for sin-offering comes from another which signifies " to make restitution for something lost," etc.

entire cultus. The belief that the offering *per se* was a meritorious act, and a magical means of propitiating the Deity and averting the penal consequences of disobedience, could not but result in the loss of the sentiment of worship and the sway of a degrading formalism, — in such a moral and spiritual degeneracy, in fact, as called forth the vehement denunciation of the Prophets.

While the acceptance of a sacrifice may be regarded from a strictly legal point of view as an acknowledgment of satisfaction, it was deemed in the Hebrew theology a modification of the law in the interest of mildness. There was found, therefore, room for mercy. God, as the Saviour of His people, is accordingly represented as forgiving sin. As inexorably severe, He is said, indeed, to visit the sins of the fathers upon the children; but in the later development of the people this doctrine is renounced. Under the law certain sins are passed by on account of sacrifices offered according to the ceremonial requirements. But the Prophets attained a higher point of view, and represented the Divine forgiveness as a free act of grace, conditioned, indeed, upon repentance and abandonment of sinful conduct. It should be kept in mind, however, that the dominant note in the Hebrew doctrine of forgiveness and salvation is deliverance from the external, temporal consequences attached to sin by the law. It would be a great error to read into this theology the ethical and spiritual apprehension of sin as a violation of the nature of man, the effects of which follow in the soul by irreversible natural law. It is arbitrary, not natural, law which is taken into account. The doctrine, however, that righteousness, obedience, and harmony with God are " good " and desirable, and that they insure peace as well as prosperity, does not fail of frequent and decided expression. In proportion as the Psalmists and Prophets rise above the earlier legalism they attain a more spiritual point of view. The theocratic conception of forgiveness and salvation was, however, scarcely transcended by any of the writers of the canonical books of the Old Testament. To them Jehovah was the God of Israel. The Divine mercy and love were for the members of the theocratic community only. Destruction would overwhelm all who were enemies of these. The hope, which finds expression in some of the Prophets, that all the ends of the earth shall see the salvation of God, could have found its expected realization only in the conversion of the heathen to the theocratic worship. The limits of particularism were not passed until Judaism came in contact with Greek culture. Whether the broadening of mind was the result of intercourse with foreign and particularly Hellenistic tendencies, or came by an inward development, may be open to question; but in the apocryphal Book of Wisdom are found conceptions of God which are closely akin to those of Jesus. He is here represented as a Spirit friendly to man. Great and small has God created, and He cares equally for all. He loves all that is, and abhors nothing which he has made; for if He hated anything He would not have created it. His imperishable spirit is in all. This noble idea may, however, very naturally have been derived from the ancient Hebrew story of the creation of man, the profound significance of which had for ages been buried under a vast system of exclusiveness and national conceit.

Under the law there was, however, a large number of sins for which no forgiveness was provided. The transgressor who had been found guilty of these could hope for no salvation. He was doomed. He must die, and this was the end as an awful warning to "those which remain." For sacrificing to Moloch, a man was condemned to be put to death by stoning. If a brother, son, daughter, wife, or friend entice a man to worship other gods, the man so enticed is ordered to "surely kill" the enticer; and the people are enjoined to stone him to death, to make his destruction sure. For blasphemy the offender, whether a native or a stranger, is doomed to death, "and all the congregation shall certainly stone him." The man who "will not hearken unto the priest" has committed an unpardonable sin and must die, that the people may " fear and do no more presumptuously." It is commanded in heart-breaking detail that the father and mother of "a stubborn and rebellious son " shall seize him and bring him as accusers to the elders of his city, that all the men of his city may stone him till he be dead.[1] The numerous curses in the

---

[1] In the twentieth chapter of Numbers is a long list of offences for which death alone could atone. The sad Book of Deuteronomy abounds in them.

twenty-eighth chapter of Deuteronomy, pronounced upon those who should not keep the
law, are equivalent to sentences of death or an-
athemas worse than death. Repulsive as all
this unmitigated severity is to a humane sentiment, it should not be overlooked that a tone
of profound moral earnestness pervades the
Old Testament; that *duty*, with whatever defects of ethical conception it may have been
apprehended, is enjoined with earnest emphasis
and endless repetition; that the will of God is
incessantly proclaimed as the supreme, invio-
lable law; that the disaster and ruin wrought
by sin are exhibited in so terrible a light as to
excite deep horror of it in the minds of the
people, and that the praises of righteousness
are sung in sweet and lofty strains. Much
easier, indeed, it is to criticise this religious
system than to invent another which could
have been established under the conditions
which determined this, or, if it had existed,
would have served the educational end which
this did undoubtedly serve.

The Hebrew conception of salvation can be
understood only in connection with the national
religious and patriotic spirit. This is true at

least of the later development of the doctrine
in the Prophets. To these great teachers Israel
appeared as the people of mankind, — a world-
people, having a providential calling which distinguished them from all other races, — and as a
mission-people in the interest of monotheistic
worship. Idolatry, all worship of other gods
than Jehovah, it is their calling to overcome,
whether in their midst or among the surround-
ing peoples. An immediate personal responsibility to God — no ceremonial intervening —
is emphasized. The heavy guilt which rests
upon the people can be removed by no sacrifice but that of sin itself, — by repentance and
return to right worship and life. The inner
law of the conscience comes in the Prophets to
clear recognition and forcible expression. The
great national mission is, however, kept constantly in view, and salvation is generally
conceived in relation to this, and as including
whatever will further this providential calling
and work, — deliverance from idolatry, from the
power of enemies, from exile and all temporal
evil, such as oppression, violence, and internal
dissension. But one personal Saviour is recognized in this prophetic teaching, and that one

is Jehovah, the all-mighty, in whose right hand is victory, and He will rear and nurture Israel as a peculiar people. For their salvation — that is, for the preservation of their national monotheistic integrity — He employs the teachings of the Prophets, misfortunes of various kinds, and especially does He scourge them with the heathen nations, whom He brings down upon them (such is the Hebrew conception of history) to lay waste and destroy, to slay and carry into exile for their disobedience and revolt. It belongs, however, to the point of view of the Prophets, while they recognize Jehovah as the true Saviour of His people, to mediate the salvation through the sufferings of the righteous, who in some sense atone for the sins of the nation. Thus the second Isaiah (chapters xl.–lxvi.) looks for the "healing" of the people by means of the "stripes" which the faithful theocratic remnant had suffered in the exile. Some of the Prophets do, however, expect a future salvation through a personal deliverer of the line of David. Out of Bethlehem should come forth one who should be "a ruler in Israel;" he should be a "rod out of the stem of Jesse," "Wonderful, Counsellor, Prince of

Peace ; " he should sit on the throne of David, restore the fallen power of the nation, and set free, cleanse, and glorify the enslaved and humiliated people. The failure of this hope to be realized in the terms in which it was conceived, illustrates the defects and limitations of the Hebrew idea of salvation, which, though occasionally showing gleams of a noble spiritual conception, was in general hampered by its theocratic point of view, and confined to an earthly and temporal scope. Under these conditions it was not adapted to become a permanent factor in a universal religion.

II. — SALVATION AS TAUGHT BY JESUS.

A doctrine of salvation appropriate to a world-religion was presented by the great Teacher, who by reason of it has earned the title of Saviour of Mankind.[1] This title will be the more readily accorded to him by all the world, the more the truly spiritual and universal character of his teaching is recognized, the more it is apprehended in its wonderful simplicity and liberated from the burden of dogma under

[1] A forthcoming volume in this series of Manuals is entitled " The Saviour of the World." — EDITOR.

which it has been for ages smothered and distorted. As a spiritual interpreter of human nature, Jesus of Nazareth has never been surpassed. As an embodiment and manifestation of whatever is noblest, purest, and tenderest in man, he stands unrivalled among the great religious teachers of the ages. Other personality so morally fruitful, so abounding in intensity of spiritual power, has never appeared in history. In him all that is most godlike and most human was united in harmony, and found consummate expression. His life is at once the enigma of the centuries and the solution of their problems. In the universality of his religious genius, in the scope and sureness of his ethical insight, in the depth of his sympathy and the breadth and lucidity of his understanding, in the intensity of his sufferings and the completeness of his victory, he was the true Son of Man. Tempted in all points, and assailed by the powers of sin and the ferocity of enraged and brutal men, he held with a firm grasp the sceptre of spiritual ascendancy which shall never depart from his hand.

Although reared in the religious faith of his people, nurtured in the law and the Prophets, Jesus recognized and adopted only the spiritual and universal principles of Hebraism and Judaism. The imperishable hope of salvation, which had been cherished in the hearts of Jews through many ages of oppression, he sought to rekindle, indeed, but only in giving it an entirely new interpretation. In the alchemy of genius all that it touches is turned into gold. Out of the spiritual crucible of Jesus the Jewish conception of salvation came forth transfigured. Now no longer did it bear its antique form of national and theocratic self-seeking, its cramped and degraded aspect of bondage to the law. Interpreting the striving and aspiration of mankind for deliverance from servitude to sin in the light of the great idea of the universal Fatherhood, he exalted salvation to the rank of a world-principle of life. Not now was it to be consummated in Jerusalem rebuilt and the magnificence of the temple restored, not in ceremony of sacrifice and voice of prayer on Gerizim, nor yet in the pitying answer to the mute despair of exiles by the rivers of Babylon, which should wake their silent harps to theocratic melodies, but in the deliverance of a world from the dominion of selfishness, in the universal reign of the kingdom of God.

1. *Relation to the Old Testament.* — The position which Jesus assumed towards the sacred
writings of the Jews, regarded both as documents of a theocratic national religion and as
literature, indicates the point of view from which
his teaching of salvation must be considered.
In the freedom of his spirit, in the grandeur of
his conception of life, and in the clearness of his
insight into the divine order of the world, he
resembled and yet surpassed the greatest of the
Prophets.   The most spiritual of these teachers
had no vision of a restored Jerusalem without
its temple and altar, which shou'd stand as
symbols not only of worship, but of national
supremacy and splendor.   But the establishment
of a political, theocratic kingdom Jesus repudi-
ated as foreign to his aim and opposed to the
spirit of his mission.   He sought to dissipate in
the minds of his followers all dreams of worldly
dominion.   As he came not to be ministered
unto, but to minister, so he taught them that in
his kingdom the position of servant was the
chief honor to be attained.   He regarded the
whole sacrificial system, the theocratic striving
and ambition, as nourishing the selfishness which
it was his mission to overcome by fostering the

spirit of universal love. To the temporal Messianic prophecies and expectations of his nation, he gave no heed and no encouragement. "My kingdom is not of this world," was his answer to the ineffectual fanaticism of those of his own time in whom the national spirit of the Prophets still excited futile strivings after political liberty and glory. He expressed no sympathy with the bondage to Rome, under which his people groaned, nor with their fruitless longing for deliverance from its chains. He even enjoined that what was due to Cæsar should be rendered to him, and did not neglect to add that duties to God must also be discharged. Not the restorer of the ancient national supremacy would he be, but the founder of a new kingdom.

In Matthew v. 17–21, Jesus makes a formal declaration of his relation to the economy of the Old Testament. As to the law or the Prophets, he came not, he says, to destroy, but to fulfil them. Not one jot or tittle of the law shall pass till all be fulfilled; and he that breaketh the least of the commandments, and teacheth men so, shall be called the least in the kingdom of heaven. Yet in the same discourse he takes a position above the law, abrogating or modifying partien-

lar commandments, and setting up his personal
authority unqualifiedly against that of " those of
old time." In respect to the law against homi-
cide he places the disposition on an equal foot-
ing with the act. As to adultery, it is within,
in the cherished lustful passion as well as in the
act contemplated in the law. The law of divorce is essentially qualified, and that of re-
taliation is abrogated, love even of enemies
being enjoined in the place of taking an eye for
an eye. The difficulty in reconciling these an-
tithetic declarations does not lie in the opposition of the general statement of Jesus that he
came to fulfil the law and the Prophets to the
free and independent position taken afterwards.
For in this very position is unmistakably indicated the manner in which he would have the
law fulfilled. In harmony with the spirit of all
his teaching, he here emphasizes the principle
that the moral quality of actions is determined
by the disposition, and that the true ethical fulfilment of the law is not in the outward act, but
in the inward feeling and intention. The fundamental opposition of his doctrine to the
legalism of the Old Testament could not be
more forcibly expressed by one who might

desire to counteract the defects of that system, while retaining whatever in it was of universal and permanent worth. But the point of hermeneutical contention is in the declaration that not one jot (the smallest Hebrew letter), nor tittle (the hook, by which nearly similar Hebrew letters are distinguished from one another), should pass till all be fulfilled, and that he who breaks the least of the commandments should be least in the kingdom of heaven. The problem is to reconcile this emphatic language of legalism and the letter with the subsequent teaching. To explain it by calling the expression hyperbolic is to evade the difficulty. For in saying that he came to fulfil the law, Jesus had already expressed himself quite fully, in a general way, and these words can indicate nothing short of an intention to set forth in most emphatic terms the legalistic point of view. They convey a universal declaration, and cannot, accordingly, be referred to his own fulfilment of the law.

The difficulties in the interpretation of the passage have led some eminent scholars to doubt that the words were spoken by Jesus, on the ground of their inconsistency with the spirit of his doctrine in general, and with his uumistakable attitude towards the legalism and literalism which they express. No solution of the difficulty which they present can probably be given which will satisfy every one. Whether by exegetical pressure they be brought into accord with what follows or be set aside as added to the tradition or the record, they must be in any case subjected to a somewhat violent treatment. For yield they must to the force of the analogy of the teaching and spirit of Jesus. His attitude in respect to the traditional legalism and the literalism of the law is indicated in his declarations regarding the Sabbath. When his disciples are censured for plucking the ears of corn on that day and he for healing the sick, he declares himself superior to the Sabbath, thus putting his personal authority against prescripts of the law. In his transfiguring of the Sabbath it becomes simply an institution to serve man, not to enslave him. Man is placed above it. It was made for him, not he for it; and he may freely use it, according to his own conscience, as it will most promote his welfare. To the complaint of the scribes and Pharisees that his disciples neglected the washing of hands before

eating, he answered that they made the law ineffectual by their traditions, and he took occa-
sion to call the multitude together and teach that
not that which enters into a man defiles him,
but that which proceeds out of his mouth, thus
showing that he regarded the Mosaic law as to
purification as morally indifferent. That he at-
tributed to the law only a relative validity is
evident from his deriving the Mosaic permission
of divorce from regard to the hardness of the
people's hearts. It is apparent, then, that he
ascribed to the law no absolute and binding authority. If he did not openly renounce it; if
he enjoined upon his followers to do whatever
the scribes and Pharisees sitting in Moses' seat
should bid them do; if he in his denunciation
of the Pharisees told them they ought to have
practised mercy and judgment, and not to have
left undone the payment of tithes of mint, anise
and cummin, — it was because he did not choose
to come to an open rupture with the law, but
believed that he had taught principles which
would in time work its dissolution and destruction and set man free from its bondage.

His treatment of the Old Testament as com-
posing the sacred writings of his nation is like-

wise remarkable, and in striking contrast to that
of his contemporaries, as Philo for example,
and to that of his followers, the evangelists.
The allegorizing of these betrays their bondage
to a theory of the infallibility of those writings,
while he put himself above them, modifying or
setting aside single prescripts, asserting his authority as Son of Man to judge for himself, to be
Lord over all institutions and the slave of none,
and declaring as the principle of his own life
and the watchword of progress for men, " It is
the spirit that quickeneth."

2. *The Ethical Factor.*—Although not openly,
yet really, setting aside the law, Jesus proceeded
in his teaching from an important point of view
of the old religion, — the moral, the practical
application of truth to the life of men. His
voice is the voice of Moses and the Prophets,
but it sounds a new note, — the note of a universal human sympathy. The present life and
the fortune of men in it hold a prominent place
in his conception of salvation. One looks in
vain through his teachings for traces of that
eager, nervous solicitude about the destiny of
the soul in another life which has unhappily
given to the popular Christian idea of salvation

a too decided tone of self-interest. That man should have his daily bread, be not led into temptation, be delivered from evil, — these were chief desiderata, aims of prayer and work. Morality is with him no trivial, secondary concern, to be put aside in the hasty pursuit of a religion valued more for its ulterior advantages than for its help in the present stress. Rather is it the foundation of his teaching. From the prominent place which morality holds in his teaching it would appear that its inculcation, the putting of it on the right ground, was thought by him to be a very important part of his mission. It was to the reform of the popular morality that he addressed himself with relentless energy from the beginning of his mission to its close. Against the hypocrisy, narrowness, and hatred, the half-heartedness, conceit, and cruelty of the dominant parties in Jewish life, he shot his sharpest words of reproof and correction. He could hardly have expressed himself in more decided and unmistakable terms, had he declared that he recognized no salvation which was not conditioned upon the recognition and practice of morality. He never disparaged this life. On the contrary, it appears to have been the underlying presumption of his teaching that the chief thing for men to do is to set themselves right with reference to their daily duties and relations towards one another. To set themselves right, — this was fundamental in the morality of Jesus, for in it everything depends on the disposition. Truthful, clean, and pure this must be, as the condition of a right life ; and all external actions find their worth determined by reference to this inward standard. Those who " draw near with their mouth and honor God with their lips " he denounces as hypocrites, after the manner of the Prophets.[1] Treasures should be laid up in heaven, because it is important that the heart, which follows the treasure, be in the right place.[2] Now, that right place can be one place only. An undivided heart is essential to a right moral life. Hence it is impossible to serve God and mammon. Singleness of heart, unity of aim, are indispensable moral requisites. If the eye be single, the whole body shall be full of light.[3] Unless the aim be undivided, the life has no promise of strength or victory. One must die to one's lower life, if one will

---

[1] Matthew xv. 7, 8.   [2] Ibid. vi. 19.   [3] Ibid. vi. 22.

truly live, — " he that loseth his life for my sake shall find it."

From this universal ethical point of view a multitude of particular and minute directions for conduct is not to be looked for. A new era in morals has begun, and the life of man is liberated from the hard restraint of arbitrary rules and left to its free development from the inward source of right belief and feeling. " Those who stood watching the career of Jesus felt that his teaching, but probably still more his deeds, were creating a revolution in morality, and were setting to all previous legislations, Mosaic or Gentile, that seal which is at once ratification and abolition. While they watched, they felt the rules and maxims by which they had hitherto lived die into a higher and larger life. They felt the freedom which is gained by destroying selfishness instead of restraining it, by crucifying the flesh instead of circumcising it. . . . It no longer seemed to them necessary to prohibit in detail and with laborious enumeration the different acts by which a man may injure his neighbor. Now that they had at heart as the first of interests the happiness of all with whom they might be brought into contact, they no longer required a law, for they had acquired a quick and sensitive instinct, which restrained them from doing harm. But while the new morality incorporated into itself the old, how much ampler was its compass! A new continent in the moral globe was discovered. Positive morality took its place by the side of Negative. To the duty of not doing harm, which may be called Justice, was added the duty of doing good, which may properly receive the distinctively Christian name of Charity. And this is the meaning of that prediction which certain shepherds reported to have come to them in a mystic song, heard under the open sky of night, proclaiming the commencement of an era of *good will to men.*"[1]

The sum of the teaching of Jesus respecting the ethical salvation of men is expressed in the celebrated principle which he declares contains all the law and the Prophets: "Whatsoever ye would that men should do to you, do ye even so to them;" which is of the same import as the direction to love one's neighbor as one's self. "Men" and "neighbor" having re-

[1] Ecce Homo, Boston, 1878, pp. 204, 205.

ceived a universal application in the interpretation of Jesus, the limits of race and social condition are removed, and the world is opened to the sympathy and interest of each individual. Since love cannot be commanded, freedom being essential to its existence, these words should be regarded as expressing the universal ethical principle of man's development, in accordance with which he can alone find his true life, his salvation from moral evil. The central ethical principle of Jesus, that the disposition is the all-important factor in conduct, finds also here its application. For if this precept be interpreted by his spirit and example, its true meaning will be seen to be nothing short of an inspiration of love and a renunciation of self, from which follows such a consecrated service of man as distinguished him whose life is expressed in the simple words, " He went about doing good."

In the moral teaching of Jesus the love of wealth and the striving for its accumulation are disapproved as endangering the higher life. Not to mention the woe pronounced upon the rich,[1] it is declared to be "the deceitfulness of riches"

[1] Luke vi. 24.

which choked the seed that fell among thorns and made it unfruitful.[1] The love of riches makes one who was inclined to follow the divine call turn back,[2] and makes another regardless of spiritual interests.[3] The service of mammon is said to be incompatible with that of God. Indeed, the claims of the kingdom of God are supreme, the ideal is high, and all lower relations and interests must yield to that which men are enjoined to "seek first." He that putteth his hand to the plough and looketh back is not fit for this kingdom of Renunciation. Love for relatives, the burying of the dead, wedding joys, — none of these must be suffered to detain him whom truth and duty call to this kingdom of Consecration. Let the dead bury the dead! If an eye or hand offend, pluck out, cut off! See that thou enter into life, though maimed and naked!

The ethical doctrine that the doing of one's duty is ample reward, that the good should not be pursued for the sake of profit or pleasure, is decidedly taught by Jesus. The reward of service, be it great or small, is a free gift,

---

[1] Matthew xiii. 22.   [2] Ibid. xix. 21-26.
[3] Luke xii. 16-20.

whether the lord of the vineyard bestow much
or little.[1] One should lend without hope of
receiving anything in return. He who has
wrought well, has at the best done no more
than his duty, and may still expect not to
regale himself, but to serve his master at sup-
per, receiving no thanks for having borne the
burden and heat of the day.[2] Whatever power
of salvation resides in morality must, indeed,
express itself according to this principle, since
on no other does conduct have any quality of
spiritual life, or even, according to Kant, any
moral quality.

The moral fruitfulness in the life, the ethically saving power of interest in the spiritual
welfare of those who by reason of weakness
have need of kindly consideration, is a fact to
which many a noble and tender character has
borne witness. Jesus, himself a fine illustration
of this spirit, enjoined it in words of great
pathos and force. The abstaining from offend-
ing the " little ones," the " cup of cold water "
borne to them, have been set forth in simple
and tender words which will be spoken of
wherever the Gospel shall be preached. " You

---

[1] Matthew xx. 1–16 ; vi. 35.   [2] Luke xvii. 7–10.

cannot step my journey for me, cannot carry
me on your back, cannot do me any *great* service ; but it makes a world of difference to me
whether I do my part in the world with or
without these little helps which fellow-travellers
can exchange."[1] It makes a world of difference to us, too, whether we tender the cup of
cold water, and, if need be, stoop to bind up the
fellow-traveller's wounds, or pass by on the
other side. Better for us were it, if we are
recreant to this duty, that a millstone be hanged
about our neck and we be cast into the sea.
The fortune of those who keep this great ethical
law is not more blessed than is the judgment of
those dreadful who break it.

3. *The Religious Factor.* — Important, however, as is the ethical factor in salvation, Jesus
did not leave the deliverance of men from sin
dependent on this alone. He had a too sure
insight, knew too well what was in man, not to
discern the human need of a higher strength
and support in the stress of temptation than
are furnished in man's moral intuitions and
sentiments, — the need of trust, faith, and hope
in a Divine Providence, — in a word, the need of

[1] W. C. Gannett.

Religion. At the centre of his teaching of religion is the idea of God as the Father of men. With him this is not, first of all, a doctrine. It is rather chiefly the expression of his profoundest feeling and belief, of his religious consciousness. He felt himself to be the Son of God, in a unique spiritual relation, but no less on this account the Son of man. His model prayer he taught to his disciples, instructing them to address his Father in heaven as theirs. Proof for the existence of the Father he seems never to have thought of asking for himself, much less of giving to others. The intimate relations of human fatherhood — its love, interest, helpfulness — are to him the earthly type of the relation of God to men, — the fatherhood which will not give a stone when asked for bread, and will extend open arms of welcome to the penitent prodigal, though returning in misery and squalor. There remains now no limitation of race. It is not the God of Abraham, Isaac, and Jacob to whom Jesus directs men, but the Universal Father. If some are the children of the evil one, it is because of their spiritual kinship; essentially they are the children of God, as He would have them spiritually be-

come. Practical in the highest degree and of
saving efficacy does this doctrine become in his
application of it to men. As children of God
they are enjoined to be perfect as He is perfect,
to strive after godlikeness, to bless those who
curse them, to love their enemies that they may
be like their Father in heaven, who maketh His
sun to shine on the evil and on the good, and
sendeth rain on the just and on the unjust.[1]
Thus does he transfigure morality into religion,
breathing into it the breath of a new life, aspiration for a divine fellowship, and the feeling
which belongs to a divine service. Thus should
men be exalted to the height of religious consciousness which he himself occupied, — the
consciousness of being children of God. So
high a religious conception as this has never
been attained by any other teacher, — a conception showing so deep an insight into the spiritual capacities and needs of man, and making a
provision so simple and so adequate for his
salvation.

That one so pure as was Jesus, living in such
high converse of spiritual fellowship with God,
should have a keen sense of sin and its dread-

[1] Matthew v. 44–48.

ful consequences in the life of man, goes without saying. His conception of his mission, his
consecration and sacrifice, find their interpretation in this. Dull of spiritual discernment,
hard of heart, having ears and hearing not,
obdurate and blind, he finds men to be, not by
reason of original depravity, but of their own
choice. As free and capable of accepting the
truth and choosing the divine life, does he always address them, with an appeal to conscience and the better impulses. As estranged
from God and in darkness, he appeals to them
to return to their allegiance and to the light.
The Father is ready to welcome them. Heaven
is moved to joy at their coming. They are
even sought with unwearied solicitude. The
shepherd is not at peace, with his ninety and
nine safely sheltered, so long as one wanders
lost. It is, indeed, these lost, bewildered souls
whom Jesus himself came to "seek and save."
The whole economy which he represents is one
of pitying tenderness, love, and mercy. Heaven
bends benignant and full of yearning over a
darkened world, to watch and support his mission. One condition is, however, imposed upon
the impenitent, — repentance ($\mu\epsilon\tau\acute{a}\nu o\iota a$), — a

change of mind, disposition, affections. To
call sinners to repentance, this Jesus declares
to be his mission.[1] Sin must, indeed, have its
dreadful course and work its inevitable anguish.
The wretched prodigal must dwell with swine
in a land seared by famine, must feel the curse
and shame of his sinful life, until he is moved to
confess that he has sinned and is unworthy to be
called a son, before the paternal clemency can be
extended to him. But when the sinner has thus
set himself right in relation to the Father ; when,
no sacrifice being required but that of his own
pride and evil passions, he has become softened
and reconciled through sorrow and suffering, —
then does forgiveness rush forth to meet him,
and he is welcomed and crowned amidst great
rejoicing as the son who was lost and is found.
What simplicity, what tenderness, what deeps
of pathos, are here ! How is the great, hard
world-order of law softened with pity and
transfigured by the touch of love !

To seek the kingdom of God and its righteousness is, according to Jesus, to attain salvation, — that is, to enter into that community of
devout souls which he came to establish on the

[1] Luke v. 32.

earth. The required righteousness must, however, exceed that of the scribes and Pharisees.
It was not the merely outward observance of
ceremonies, but an inward likeness to God.
This righteousness was a new religious idea as
apprehended and taught by him, an old principle
transformed ; for in it the old separation of man
and God is removed, and the human soul re-
nounces its will and gives itself up in love and
trust to the Father. They who hunger and
thirst after righteousness are among the blessed,
for they shall be filled. In fellowship with
God, in the God-consciousness, as he knew it,
shall they find peace and everlasting strength.
Let them take his soft yoke and easy burden,
and they shall have rest, not only from weari-
some ceremony and hollow formalism, but also
from the fatal bondage of sin, and with him
enter into liberty and life in God. A light
yoke and an easy burden ! Strange paradox !
Wondrous invitation ! This sorrowful and bur-
dened soul, this great cross-bearer, invites men
to come to him for rest ! Yet the resolving of
this paradox reveals the secret of salvation as
discerned and taught by Jesus. In communion
with God, in the sense of not being alone be-

cause the Father is with him, in love, trust, and
faith, in doing righteousness with singleness of
heart, in fulfilling a divine mission although
uncomprehended and abandoned by the world,
a man in mortal weakness and shaken by temptation finds an invincible strength. The yoke
of such a service is soft to his neck; the heaviest
cross, an easy burden.

This coming to him, this prominence given
to his personality, is a unique feature in Jesus'
teaching of salvation, — a feature which places
his interpreters in the dilemma of either charg-
ing him with the most audacious assumption,
or admitting that he was profoundly conscious
of holding to men the relation of exhibiting
an ideal type of life, in the appropriation of
which salvation was pre-eminently, if not alone,
to be found. The everlasting or eternal life,
the idea of which is central in his conception
of the saving of men from sin, he represents
as manifested in himself, as to be communicated
to the world through his personality. This
divine life-principle, by which the earthly existence of man is transfigured and glorified, the
life in faith and love and spiritual striving, is
to be attained by belief in him. " He that

believeth on the Son hath everlasting life," is a great saying which no magical interpretation can exhaust ; but it must be understood in the light of the declaration that it hath been given to the Son to have life in himself as the Father hath it in Himself. To acquire eternal life by faith in Jesus is, accordingly, to believe in his life of consecration, obedience, worship, and love, and make it one's own. The simplicity and directness of the process of salvation as thus taught by Jesus, compared with the complicated " plan of salvation " as set forth in Christian theology, call to mind Lessing's distinction between the Christian religion and the religion of Christ.[1]

By the life of Jesus, however, by the power of his personality as manifesting truth, are men to be saved, according to his teaching, and not by means of his death. To come to him, to follow him, to keep the commandments, to renounce earthly possessions, to seek the kingdom of God, — these things must he do who would have eternal life. In his Sermon on the Mount, in his discourses generally before

[1] " Lessing's Theological Opinions," Universalist Quarterly, April, 1881.

his departure from Cæsarea Philippi for Judæa, there are no allusions to a connection between his death and his work as Saviour; and nowhere do we find him teaching that belief in his death or in any effects to be wrought by his death has a saving efficacy. One passage, however, presents some difficulty, and a difference of opinion has arisen in its interpretation. In Matthew xx. 28, Jesus says that he "came not to be ministered unto, but to minister, and to *give his life a ransom for many.*" But there is here no mention of faith in his death, nor of any subjective appropriation of it as a means of salvation. To his death are, indeed, ascribed the meaning and effect of a ransom, — for as implying his death, we ought probably to interpret the words " to give his life." The interpretation hinges on the meaning which belongs to " ransom." · The original meaning is " price for redeeming;" and if it is to be taken strictly in that sense, here it can only mean that one life, that of Jesus, was given and accepted in the place of the lives of many, that is, to save them from death. But the connection, as well as the whole analogy of his teaching, appears to require the interpretation that his death, like his life, is to be regarded as saving, delivering, setting free morally and spiritually from bondage to sin. That the connection favors the ethical and not the legalistic interpretation, is evident from this, that there the ministering quality, the service, of his life is made the central idea of his mission. It is in this way that he releases, or ransoms, men. His death, the crowning act of this service, is just such a λύτρον, or "ransom." [1]

[1] Winer and Meyer, the highest grammatical authorities, lay stress upon the preposition ἀντί, which, as here used, means "instead of;" and the latter maintains that *substitution* is expressed by it here. Baur takes this view also, and regards the words as not spoken by Jesus, so strongly does he think them opposed to the analogy of the teaching of the Gospels. On the contrary, De Wette says that "ransom" is not to be taken as indicating an exchange, but *dynamically* as marking an effect. The passage is no doubt difficult, and grammar appears to come into conflict with analogy of teaching in its interpretation. But the question may fairly be raised whether or no it is not *hypergrammatical* to attempt, as Meyer does, to establish a doctrine upon a single preposition in writings composed as the Gospels were, and having had such a fortune as they have had in the hands of copyists, — more especially when the words in question were undoubtedly spoken in another language than that in which they were written down in the record. In this case one will surely not be accused of hermeneutical violence in making the preposition yield to the analogy.

III. — THE PAULINE DOCTRINE.

Jesus died upon the cross; but the greatest of his followers saw in that instrument of torture the glorified central figure in a universal plan of salvation, and gave it a unique interpretation for the ages. Saul of Tarsus, reared in the traditions of Judaism and according to the tenets of the strictest of its sects, learned in Rabbinical lore, a student of the law and the Prophets, a zealot in his religion, a persecutor of the Christians, was suddenly converted to the religion of Jesus while on his way to Damascns as its most dreaded enemy. Upon the details of this conversion it is not necessary here to enter, nor to discuss its probable preparations and antecedents. It is enough that Saul, the persecutor of Christianity, became Paul, its greatest apostle; for as an apostle, or one sent, he regarded himself from the eventful hour of his conversion. From that hour he gloried in the cross, which before he had looked upon as the detestable symbol of a noxious fanaticism. Now rather did it have for him a world-historical significance, and stand for the breaking down of partition walls of Judaistic national exclusiveness, for the abolishing of distinctions of race and sect in relation to the Divine favor, for the universal offer of the Divine grace to men, and for universal liberty and salvation. Although it might be to the Jew a stumbling-block and to the Greek foolishness, to this seer it was " the power of God."

The great Apostle to the Gentiles, properly so called because he apprehended Christianity as a universal principle, takes as the central thought of his Gospel the idea of Righteousness, that " master-impulse of Hebraism." The relation of man to God — or, in other words, religion — he brings under this conception. The fitness, the rightness, in this relation; conformity to God's will; " harmony with the universal order;" the state of mind which God will have in men, — are all expressed by this great word. To him the task of religion is to bring men into this relation, and its great problem is how to do it. Now, if he had been dealing with religion in general, it is evident that his discussion of the question would have taken a very wide range, and we should not have had what may very properly be called his distinctive contributions to religion, or what he calls his " Gospel."

It is, however, as a Christian that he approaches
the problem, and as a Christian it is that with
masterly insight he seizes upon the personal factor which, as we have seen, Jesus made so conspicuous. For him righteousness is no mere
abstraction. It has had once for all, for all
ages and for all men, a perfect embodiment and
manifestation. It has been lived; and in the
life which had revealed it he sees the whole
meaning which Christianity has for him, his
sole hope for personal deliverance from sin and a
universal principle and power for the salvation
of the world. Of his own spiritual transformation, or conversion, he says it is a revelation of the Son of God in him which it has
pleased God to make.[1] Hereby has come into
his life and into that of every Christian a new
religious consciousness, in which there are no
more the bondage and limitations of Judaism,
but liberty and a spiritual principle victorious
over the flesh. The spirit ($\pi\nu\epsilon\acute{u}\mu a$) it is which
the Christian has received, and whereby he is
distinguished from what he was before, whether
Jew or Gentile. They who receive Christ into
their life by faith receive this spirit; for he, the

[1] Galatians i. 15, 16.

Lord, is spirit,[1] and where the spirit of the Lord is, there is liberty. No longer now is their salvation dependent on aught external, but it is conditioned on fellowship and union with God. In receiving the Son, they themselves become sons of God; for this spirit which they have had revealed in them, this Christ-principle, is the spirit of adoption whereby they cry, "Abba, Father."

The absolute necessity of the mediation of Christ in man's attainment of righteousness, in his justification or salvation, is the great thesis of the Pauline soteriology. Of the two kinds of righteousness which the Apostle recognizes, that of "works" and that of "faith," the former is declared to be unattainable. This is legal righteousness, or righteousness under the law, which, so far as Jews were concerned, could be attained only by fulfilling the Mosaic law, and so far as the heathen were concerned, by following the law "written in their hearts." It is the righteousness of obedience, of entire fulfilment of the law, whereby alone from this point of view man can come into the required relation to God. That man cannot fulfil the

[1] 2 Corinthians iii. 17.

law, and hence can never compass the righteousness which is of works, is the fundamental
proposition of Paul for this negative side of his
doctrine of salvation.   His own profound consciousness of sin should doubtless not be left
out of account in appreciating his judgment on
this point. But why is the law thus ineffectual?
It is through the law that the consciousness of
sin comes: " the law is spiritual; " it is " holy,
right, and good." [1]   How, then, is that whose
" design was life " found to " issue in death "?
The answer to this is found in Paul's conception of the " flesh," — a term by which he
designates not the body only, but the sensuous,
earthly nature of man, which is prone to sin, —
in a word, all that is opposed to the "spirit." It
is the seat and organ of sin.   In this lies the
reason of the inability of the law to "make
alive." It is " weak through the flesh." [2]   The
imperative of the law, its high ideal, its conviction of sin, are ineffectual against this fatal
power, this fleshliness, this tendency to sin.
But is there not " the law of the mind," or
reason, " the inner man," to contend against the
flesh? The fact that the Apostle recognizes this

[1] Romans vii. 7–17.   [2] *Ibid.*, viii. 3.

principle in the unregenerate man, this mind which " delights in the law of God," shows how far he was from the Augustinian point of view in his anthropology, — from the doctrine of the fall of man and hereditary depravity. Yet the " mind " is unable with the law and with experience to prevail against the flesh ; and the " wretched man," after all his ineffectual struggle, at the end of the pathetic conflict is brought "into captivity to the law of sin."

Here, from the Apostle's point of view, would man be left, weak, defeated, hopeless, were it not for Christ, who alone could redeem him ; or rather, were it not for the grace of God in Christ. " For what the law could not do," what the " inner man," or the reason, " the law of the mind," was unable to do in its endless and ineffectual struggle with the flesh, " God hath done, who on account of sin sent His own son .·.. and passed sentence of condemnation on sin in the flesh ; so that what is required by the law is accomplished in us who walk not according to the flesh, but according to the spirit." [1] Thus is salvation placed by Paul in immediate dependence on the person of Christ, who is a

[1] Romans viii. 1–4.

means employed by the Father for enabling man
to acquire the righteousness which shall put
him into relations of harmony and peace with
God. The old order has passed away. The
law is abrogated in the sense that its requirements possess a power to effect righteousness.
Man cannot be justified by the works of the
law, because *without Christ* he is unable to
render a perfect obedience. We have not, however, here an artificial scheme, nor a scheme of
salvation by magic, nor yet the Augustinian one
of "satisfaction." Paul does not degrade Christ
to the place of a victim sacrificed to appease the
wrath of God. It is contrary to the whole
temper of the Apostle's mind and the whole tone
of his teaching, that a man should come to so
great a fortune as that of righteousness through
the fiction of appropriating the merits of Christ.
To manifest the righteousness of God is the
death of His Son set forth, and the " propitiation " is a mere reference to Jewish ceremonial,
and must not be pressed, since it has no vital
connection with Paul's real doctrine of salvation.
So precious an offering as this blameless life,
and nothing less than this, is, indeed, well
adapted to manifest the Divine sense of the

enormity of sin, against which the Divine righteousness is relieved in glaring contrast. But to Paul the death of Christ had its chief significance for men. Upon them was its effect. The great Martyr on the cross turned his face, distorted with agony, not towards the unrelenting heavens to affect the Deity, but upon the earth for the sake of men. Accordingly, Paul declares that " God was in Christ, reconciling the world unto Himself." That God needed to be reconciled to men, seems never to have entered his mind. In his death, the destruction of his flesh, Christ is manifested to Paul as spirit and as spiritualizing. Now that he has passed through the great transformation and even the great victory, he is no longer to Paul the material, temporal. limited Messiah of the Jews, but a universal spiritual and quickening power. If he has ever known Christ after the flesh, he says, he now so knows him no longer, since he has died for all ; nor will he henceforth know any man after the flesh, since, Christ having died for all, all have died, their death to the flesh being included in his dying on their behalf.[1] Here, indeed, we have a " substitution," and the only substitution

[1] 2 Corinthians v. 14–15.

which Paul knows. Christ, dying on behalf of all, typifies in his death the death of all men to the flesh and to sin, " that they should no longer live to themselves, but to him who died for their sakes."

As a representative of the race, then, it is that, in Paul's view, Christ in his life and in his death stands forth; yet not as a representative of the race only, but as one who loved all men and would bring them all to his own spiritual attainment. In his life he had been a perfect manifestation of " the righteousness of God," and thus an ideal set up for men and *a quickening spirit*. In his death all men died to sin, and the world was ideally reconciled to God; that is, men assumed such a relation to Him as to be proper subjects of the forgiveness which He was always ready to grant. No longer does the law overshadow them with its antique and awful aspect of bondage. Christ has rendered it a perfect fulfilment, being without sin. " The handwriting of ordinances that was against us " he has " nailed to the cross," and now the level way of salvation lies open to men through participation in the life and power of his triumphant spirit.

One factor is yet, however, wanting to effect

the great work of men's salvation through Christ.
The righteousness to be attained is that through
faith. This faith, as Paul apprehends it, is as
far as possible removed from magic and mystery.
It does not effect a transfer of the " merits " of
Christ to man. It is belief in the whole manifestation by Christ of the higher life, of the spirit,
— belief in his death and resurrection. They
who believe in Christ are one with him; with
him they have died, having crucified the flesh,
and with him have they risen to newness of life.
" Faith is the bond," says a great interpreter of
Paul,[1] " of a fellowship of life with Christ, in
which Christ so lives in us that all which in us
is only limited, only belongs to our selfish ego,
is removed, and we no longer live to ourselves,
but in him." In the same vein writes one of
the acutest literary interpreters of the Apostle:[2]
" Identifying ourselves with Christ through this
attachment [of faith], we become as he was; we
live with his thoughts and feelings, and we participate, therefore, in his freedom from the ruin-
ous law in our members, in his obedience to
the saving law of the spirit, in his conformity to
the eternal order, in the joy and peace of his

[1] F. C. Baur. [2] Matthew Arnold.

life in God." Faith does not, however, effect this consummation alone. It "works by love," by recognition of and response to that divine principle to which was due the sending of Christ, and his own offering up of himself for men. Without this, faith could not bring about that entire union with Christ in which we participate in his self-sacrificing spirit, die with him to the selfish lusts of the flesh, and have a share also in his victory.

Is there, then, no place for works, for the law, for morality in this scheme of the Apostle? Far be it! They who so apprehend him as to answer this question in the affirmative do not know his profundity, his practical sense. They forget that he was of the Hebrew stock, pre-eminent in its genius for righteousness. They suppose him to have mistaken entirely the practical morality of Jesus, to have misconceived the whole spirit and method of his Master. This polemic against the law, this panegyric of faith, are but the strong contrasting of Judaism and Christianity, and do not affect, much less invalidate, the conceptions of duty, obedience, and service. He did not so misunderstand the religion of his nation as to regard it as altogether

legalistic and external, as taking no account of
the disposition and finding no place for pardon.
A stern moralist in his judgment of himself, he
never loses sight of the moral law and human
responsibility. We accordingly find him declaring with solemn emphasis that God will
render to every one according to his works, and
proclaiming that tribulation and distress shall
be upon every soul whose works are evil. Works
and faith together are the two essential factors
in attaining righteousness. With what unwearied energy did he spend himself in the service
of his Master and of men! To him the union
of the soul with Christ through faith was a
partaking of the Christ-spirit of consecration to
toil, to the dungeon, to stripes, or to the cross
for the sake of men. The righteousness of faith
was consummated in the righteousness of loving
service and all-renouncing sacrifice.

IV. — The Doctrine in Hebrews.

The Epistle to the Hebrews, the author of
which is unknown, presents the doctrine of salvation from a peculiar point of view. Whether
the writer was influenced, as some hold, by
the Alexandrian philosophy or not, he un-

questionably held a view of the relation of Judaism to Christianity quite different from Paul's.
In Paul the two are related as letter and spirit,
servitude and sonship; in this writer, as pre-
figuration and completion, as shadow and reality.
The Epistle was evidently written for Jews,
with the design of showing them that Christianity was a fulfilment of things typified in
the old religion, and of making easy their transi-
tion from the one to the other. Interest in this
writing, so far as it relates to salvation, centres
in its apprehension of the office of Christ,
which is here treated under the conception of
the priesthood. Christianity is a completion
of the Jewish religion, that "shadow of things
to come," in the dignity and grandeur of its
priestly, atoning institution. A "Priest forever, after the order of Melchizedec," Christ
assumed the sacrificial office, and " once for all "
entered into the sanctuary, and " with his own
blood obtained for us everlasting redemption."
Into no sanctuary made with hands, however,
did he enter, but "into heaven itself, now to
appear in the presence of God in our behalf."
Unpauline as is this transfer of the scene of
Christ's work from earth to heaven, there is a

reminiscence of the doctrine of Paul as to the reconciling efficacy of Christ's offering of himself in the fine words : " How much more shall the blood of Christ, who by his *everlasting spirit* offered himself without spot to God, *purify your conscience from dead works*, for the worship of the living God ! " From the point of view of this writer the work of Christ consists chiefly in consummating an atoning work shadowed forth in the ceremonial of the Old Testament. Depreciated as a " shadow," the old economy is exalted by the very fact of its prefiguring function. The Epistle contains no reference to the Pauline contrast of the righteousness of faith and of works, and faith itself receives an interpretation quite different from Paul's absolute trust in the saving grace of God in Christ. Far from being set forth as a distinctively Christian virtue, examples of its exercise are drawn from Jewish history or legend. It is declared to be " the substance of things hoped for, a conviction of things not seen." Not as a mystic fellowship of the life with Christ is it taught or illustrated, but rather as a holding fast to supersensible things, a looking for that " city which hath founda-

tions" whose builder and maker is God, and
for that " better and heavenly country." The
exaltation of the priestly, atoning office of Christ
in this Epistle, and its implied depreciation of
the present life, may suggest an -inquiry as to
the extent of its influence in shaping a long
prevailing type of Christian theology. Too
much, perhaps, have men interpreted the New
Testament by this work of an unknown author
which did not even find a place in the Canon
without decided opposition.

V. — SALVATION AND SCIENCE.

Mr. Huxley, in one of his Lay Sermons, ex-
presses a preference for justification by verification over justification by faith. The inference
which one would naturally draw from this expression is that the sort of justification which
Mr. Huxley prefers is, in the opinion of a representative of science, a real, scientific justification, while the other is unsubstantial, imagi-
nary, — in a word, unscientific. Now, to brand
an opinion or process as unscientific is, in these
days, in the opinion of very many people, to put
upon it the seal of condemnation and annulment. It may, accordingly, be well to give a

little space in this monograph on Salvation to the inquiry whether or no there is, after all, an irreconcilable difference between these two ways of attaining righteousness, and whether Mr. Huxley's placing of them in so sharp a contrast is not due to his misapprehension of the real nature of the latter. As to verification, no one knows better than they who are greatly occupied with it that far from being in any way opposed to faith, it is so much dependent thereon that without it it cannot proceed at all. Every process of the kind depends upon putting trust in certain ultimate principles which, if not intuitively discerned and hence requiring faith in the immediate declarations of the human consciousness, are the products of human experience through many ages, and as such call for belief in the integrity of the nature of man. That much depends, too, in the construction of any science, on the trustworthiness of human testimony, every scientific investigator will concede. All the great sciences are the accumulations of the contributions of observers and students often unknown to one another and separated by great intervals of time or space. How much depends, likewise, on the sureness of an eye or a hand, the accuracy of perception, the correctness of inference, and the freedom from bias in the observer, is very apparent. The great authorities in science, men of creative power, whose genius marks epochs in knowledge, are objects of faith, one might almost say of worship, to their followers. What yawning chasms would open in the continuity of science if one could no longer have faith in the sure insight and conscientious accuracy of a Newton or a Darwin! A lapse of faith in its conspicuous authorities would work such confusion and catastrophe in the world of science as doubt of the integrity and truth of Jesus would cause in the Christian Church. Moreover, faith as a factor in scientific verification has yet another application. Will any one deny that faith in a great master in science, in the sense of a trustful appropriation to one's self of his spirit, his enthusiasm, his devout consecration to truth, and his sympathy with Nature, — in a word, a fellowship of life with him, — might be vastly helpful to a disciple?

If, now, verification is not carried on without faith, or at least if faith is a very important factor in it, it would appear to follow that the justification by verification which Mr. Huxley advocates is also not without relation to faith. He who should undertake to acquire righteousness by verification, that is, by scientifically or experimentally establishing the ethical and spiritual principles on which it rests, would evidently be greatly aided by faith, and in particular by that application of it in which he might adopt as his own the virtues, the spirit, and the enthusiasm whereby a great Master of Righteousness had triumphed. On the other hand, the justification by faith, which modern science regards as unreal and sentimental, will be found, when stripped of the magic which has so long disguised it, to proceed quite in the manner of verification, and to be in fact a sort of righteousness according to science. For to live conformably to verified principles, whether in the sphere of the physical life or of the soul, is to live scientifically. Whoever, then, pursues righteousness, trusting in a great moral and spiritual order, which experience has verified as the true order for human beings, and conformity to which has been found for many ages to render the lives of men strong, sweet, and noble, is, though not far from the kingdom of

Heaven, still within the realm and method of
science. And it is, surely, no unscientific proceeding to take, as Paul did, a great principle
illustrated in a great life as the basis for a philosophy of living, and to carry out the pursuit
of righteousness in conformity with it. The
dash of mysticism in his idea of identification
with Christ in his death does not invalidate his
essentially scientific position, which is that a
mode of life which has been verified and shown
to be of the noblest sort is, therefore, to be commended and trustingly adopted. Even as to
this matter of dying, which Paul puts in a
mystical way, — is it not, after all, in the highest
sense scientific, that is, verifiable, that he who
will live to the higher things must die to the
lower? One would scarcely presume to say
that Jesus was dealing with an unreality, an
image of the fancy, and not rather with a most
substantial, not to say awful fact, when he as-
serted that he who would save his life must lose
it. Do not even the scientists the same, — that
is, die to indolence, prejudice, and the senses,
that they may live to the truth, to reason, to
discovery? No one, assuredly, will charge the
great Goethe with being unscientific, and it is

he whom Mr. Arnold regards as "an nnsus-pected witness to the psychological and sci-entific profoundness of Paul's conception of life and death."[1] "Die and 1e-exist!" he says; "for so long as this is not accomplished, thou art but a troubled guest upon an earth of gloom." ·

It may very well be imagined, however, that Mr. Huxley would say that Paul did not con-fine himself to the sphere of the verifiable, but included God in his scheme, teaching that sal-vation is by His grace in Christ. Now, from the point of view of science, God is not verifiable, and the grace of God is a fiction with which it can have nothing to do. But the scientific character of Paul's method of justification by faith is not affected by his conception of a Being from whom, as he assumed, proceeded the order of spiritual phenomena and laws with which he was dealing. The relating of these to an ulti-mate Power which he could not explain, neither supports nor invalidates the interpretation of them in relation to the particular end, — righ-teousness, or justification. Science, too, has its ultimate powers and principles, which it does not

[1] Saint Paul and Protestantism, London, 1870, p. 149.

pretend to account for or comprehend. Yet its particular relatings of phenomena and inductions of laws proceed with as much certainty as if it had fathomed the unknowable, or could give an account of the nature of matter or force. If science were without faith and righteousness without verification and a scientific basis, then might there be, indeed, an irreconcilable discord between these two most powerful and most fruitful agencies in human development.

VI. — SECULAR SALVATION.

It has already been intimated in the foregoing section that if Salvation were stripped of the disguise of magic which has been put upon it, it would be found to have points of relation with science otherwise unobserved. It may fairly be presumed, .too, that when thus revealed in its real nature it will be seen to have more to do with this world, to stand in more relations to the secular life of men, than has commonly been supposed. From the magical point of view it has generally been understood to be a means of escaping, or a condition of having escaped, the penalties of the violated law of God, — safety, refuge from the storm of Divine wrath which it

was supposed would especially break forth in the
life to come. Thus the chief interest in salvation has been centred in its relations to that life,
and it has been given a predominant other-
worldly tone. Now, it has already been pointed
out how much stress was laid by Jesus on conduct, and how Paul, notwithstanding his vigorous polemic against the law, still attached the
greatest importance to righteousness in the
sense of the right relation of man to the Divine
order, regardless of worlds, whether of this or
some other, and of times and eternities. In
order, then, that the pursuit of salvation be not
degraded so as to become chiefly an eager, selfish seeking for a remote and undefined good,
and a hasty scramble for security from some
other-world peril, it would seem that all sound
thinking and healthy feeling concerning it must
assume a decidedly this-world tone. Not that
the life to come, that destiny, is of no interest
and importance, but that it is of supreme importance to right conduct that men lay slighter
stress upon times and places and far more upon
moral and spiritual relations, and believe that
righteousness .attained and held fast in this
present life will open to its possessor all the

mansions of the Father's house. The real danger to which theology is exposed is not that of becoming too practical, but that of being turned into a theurgy. So soon as the chief interest in righteousness is transferred from this earthly theatre of man's struggle and temptation, and concentrated upon future security, theology becomes degraded to the rank of a system of magic, the show of which man may, indeed, be interested in watching, but such a theology will touch his life only a little more than any common jugglery. It is not the theurgy of the now departing theology which has nurtured great characters, but the practical morality, the simple faith of Jesus, and the tender but majestic life which the Gospels make known.

If, now, the conception of salvation ought to be extended so much as to include the deliverance of man from all that binds him in the stress and struggle of his earthly life, from all that hinders his attainment of righteousness here, then there should be included among its agencies many of what may be called the secular factors or forces. If his life does not consist in the abundance of the things which he possesses, neither does it consist in their paucity. Since it is his fortune to work out his own salvation, he may well rejoice in having unlimited means and agencies at his disposal, for it is ordained that he shall not do this in his closet nor in the desert, but in the midst of men. His nature is so complex, its several faculties are so dependent on one another in their development, that a well-ordered adjustment and harmony of all is essential to the true culture of any. To isolate any one of his faculties in its training is like the folly of applying special cultivation to one branch of a vine and leaving the stock in wildness and weeds. The true salvation is that of the entire man. It is the harmony of his whole nature with the great order of things in which it is placed. The salvation of the "soul" is a misnomer borrowed from the vocabulary of magic. Let us know henceforth only the salvation of man, — a healthy soul in a healthy body. A right theory of salvation requires a sound anthropology no less than a sound theology. To our peril do we leave physiology and hygiene out of the account. Paul, with his keen practical sense, saw the importance of this physical side of man to a true soteriology, and did not fail to take the body into his system of righteousness. "I so fight," he says, " not as one striking the air, but I beat down my body and bring it into subjection."[1] To him, as to every right-thinking person, the whole nature of man is sacred, and each part is to be regarded with awe. The body is " the temple of the Holy Spirit,"[2] — a holy place for the worship of the soul. " Therefore," he exclaims, " glorify God in your body." By no hot-house methods with a single faculty did he look for fruitage. " Present your bodies a living sacrifice." How, indeed, like one vainly striking the air, does he appear who with eager, nervous haste pursues the phantom of salvation for his " soul," while body, intellect, and moral faculty remain in sad neglect as having no share in the Divine fortune of righteousness. The sturdy Apostle may very well have wrought out his salvation in part by beating down his body. The problem may, however, be approached from another side, and we may find our secular salvation promoted by such a training of the body as shall render it the ready servitor of the soul in its attainment of the higher life, — no longer a weight, but a support.

---

[1] 1 Corinthians ix 26, 27.   [2] Ibid., vi. 19.

The principle, then, of this secular branch of our theme is that all the physical, intellectual, and ethical forces which contribute to the development of human nature, to the upbuilding of man, should be taken into account and utilized in the working out of his salvation, and that the conception of salvation should be enlarged so as to include all these. The conduct of education, the making of laws, the establishment and direction of institutions, the observance of social amenities and courtesies, ethical training, sanitary and hygienic regulations, the momentous struggle against intemperance, the striving for political honesty and purity, the humane ministries of charity, aspirations and efforts in the interest of brotherhood and universal peace and good-will, — these and their kindred, whose name is legion, should be regarded and employed as agencies in compassing human salvation, — that is, in making man complete. The religion which leaves these out of account may, indeed, be a fine celestial scheme, but it is not a religion for men, and will not long endure upon the earth.

VII. — The Intelligent, Emotional and Voluntary Factors.

In the fourth Gospel Jesus is reported to have said, " Ye shall know the truth, and the truth shall make you free." This recognition by the highest authority of an intelligent factor in salvation may well claim our attention, more especially since, in the current expositions of the doctrine, it is too much disregarded. The conception of salvation as a growth proceeding according to the laws of the mind brings this factor into prominence, and assigns it its true value. Subject to these laws, the process of salvation may very well be assumed to take the natural order,— that is, the order in which knowledge has the precedence. The difference between the product which is called salvation and the product which we may name any other mental state does not consist so much in the difference of its factors as in that of the subject matter. The condition in question is a peculiar state of the will and feelings resulting from the occupation of the knowing faculty, or the intelligence, with a peculiar kind of facts, or truths. Salvation is the overcoming of tendencies, passions, influences, temptations, which are contrary to the laws of the nature of man, the putting of one's self in harmony with these laws, and the persistent, consecrated living in accordance with them. It is something more than this. It is conformity with this order as a Divine order, as proceeding from and imposed by a Heavenly Father, a striving for obedience to and fellowship with Him in faith. Now, the particular order of facts with which the intelligence is occupied in the course of this process may be generally characterized as moral and spiritual, — facts and laws which relate to conduct and the religious life. A clear perception and a right knowledge and relating of these are the first and indispensable requisite, without which the appropriate feelings and volitions are impossible. With knowledge, then, salvation evidently begins. First of all, man must find himself, his position and relations, in the great order of which he is a part. He must recognize himself as a spiritual and responsible being, acknowledge the Power above, and know the fruitful words of prophet, seer, or Christ. Jesus appears to have laid so much stress upon knowledge as to declare that eternal life

consists in knowing God and the Son whom He
has sent. This knowledge may, assuredly, be
regarded as inclusive enough, and, if had with
the requisite intensity, as likely to produce the
feelings and volitions appropriate to the state
of salvation.

Important, however, as are knowledge, education, and instruction, these are ineffectual
without the emotional and voluntary factors.
Knowledge is not power. It is only one of the
conditions of power. Neither is it salvation,
but merely a condition of it. The beatitude
is not pronounced on those who know righteousness, but on those who hunger and thirst for
it. The product of intelligence, the material
of knowledge, is supplied in vain unless the
emotional, affectional, and voluntary powers —
the great motive forces — perform their part.
The prominence given to love in the teachings
of Christ is not without profound significance,
— love to God being made of supreme moment
in religion, and love to man in morality. We
have seen, too, how Paul, a profound psycholo-
gist as well as theologian, accentuated the emotional factor in connection with faith in Christ.
It is not irreverent, let us hope, and certainly

not irrelevant, to cite here the testimony of an eminent scientist and philosopher: "Already we have seen that the connection is between action and feeling; and hence the corollary that only by a frequent passing of feeling into action is the tendency to such action strengthened. . . . Not by precept, though heard daily; not by example, unless it be followed; but only by action, often caused by the related feeling, can a moral habit be formed."[1] Well did Paul feel the weakness of the law against the flesh and the profound need of a "quickening spirit" to effect the deliverance of man from bondage to his lower nature. .What is it but infirmity of will which speaks in the pathetic cry of the "wretched man" for rescue from "the body of this death"? So far as education may contribute to salvation, it is evident that it must address itself as well to the emotions and the will as to the intelligence. Each man's duty to himself and to those whom he may influence is to bring these great motive forces as much as possible under influences and discipline favorable to moral and spiritual development.

[1] Herbert Spencer, Study of Sociology, New York, 1882, p. 367.

The freedom of the will confers upon man, subject of course to influences, the fearful power of determining his own destiny. The pathetic words of Jesus, " But ye would not," are a solemn recognition of this fact. In this life, certainly, and in any life in which man retains his identity, the choice of good or evil is his and his alone. Salvation cannot, assuredly, be forced upon him, neither can he be kept in a state of sin and condemnation if he choose it not. The power of the keys is in his own hand. Himself may he bind or loose; for himself, open any door of darkness or of light. Not without some appearance of reason, accordingly, has doubt been thrown upon the dogmatic affirmation of the salvation of any or of all. Good reasons there were, indeed, for this doubt, if man's choices were alone to be taken into the account. But while man is free, he is not abandoned. The unrelenting powers of Truth and Light have a hold upon him and the infinite persuasions of Love forsake him not. His deathless conscience, with its eternal protest and inexorable demands, testifies to the preponderance of good in himself. Not only does the Eternal beset him behind and before and lay His hand upon him, but God is immanent in man, and there is hope of the transformation of every deformed soul into the Divine likeness so long as God is.

VIII. — "Probation" and Morals.

The conclusion which must be drawn from the foregoing section is that salvation is subject to the law of cause and effect, — a law of which psychology as well as physics has to take account. Certain psychological conditions or causes, certain factors of knowledge, feeling, and will, are the necessary antecedents of the condition called salvation. Deliverance from sin implies a conviction of it; a perception of the law of which it is the violation; repentance towards God, the author of the law; a hunger and thirst after righteousness and a resolute will to attain it. When these factors are operative, the state of soul which they condition invariably follows, unless counteracting causes intervene. In the absence of these factors of life, other factors, those of moral and spiritual death, are in operation, bringing forth with fatal certainty their appropriate product. Therefore, each successive state of the soul, each expression of its

strength or weakness, is dependent on, and in
a sense determined by, antecedent conditions,
— power begetting power, obedience bringing
forth life, and disobedience bringing forth death.
Accordingly, under the operation of the law of
causation, man is perpetually in a state of probation ; that is, his conduct to-day determines
in a measure the moral and spiritual conditions
under which to-morrow's conflict must be entered upon.   To-day, yesterday's defeat or victory contributes its influence in depression and
despair, or in uplifting and hope. Every success
in the endless moral struggle makes subsequent
success easier, and every failure makes it more
difficult.   To say this is to affirm that character
is a constant factor in spiritual development;
that as it is, namely, has been made by antecedent choices, it determines in a large degree
the effect of influences, instruction, circum-
stances which may be brought to bear upon
men. Probation so conceived is interminable,
and of course never comes to a fixed or final
condition.   There is no period in it at which
action and responsibility cease and judgment
begins. Judgment proceeds hand in hand with
action, since every deed is a cause on which its

effect or judgment follows under unchangeable law. There is, there can be, no " final judgment" for a soul to whose activity no final limit is set.

Now, it is evident that in probation thus regarded all the moral forces have their due place and influence. Character is recognized as an indefeasible possession, and responsibility continues unbroken. Every act of obedience, service, fidelity, or of disobedience and falsity, has its legitimate effect. All attainment of excellence is an increment of the soul's moral stature or strength. Inexorable justice has its course, no artificial scheme interfering to cheat it of its claims. Man is lulled to no false security, and is not taught to trifle with the law. God is not mocked. The same unchangeable laws prevail so long as the soul exists in this life and that to come. The course of character is continuous, regardless of time and scene. All the moral influence and all the stimulus and support which accrue from a sense of the inviolability of the moral order, from the conviction that what is gained belongs forever to him who will hold it, and what is lost must be regained by arduous struggle, remain in force unimpaired. Virtue

is encouraged by the assurance that it belongs
to God's eternal order, and that all which is
mighty and all which is good in the universe
contends for and with it. Vice is not encouraged by the fallacious teaching that through a
scheme of substitution it can evade the law, and
by a tardy repentance sustain a claim to parade
in the garments of virtue. There is fixed no
period of time at which all that the soul has
gained by fidelity may be lost by reason of not
having fulfilled certain conditions, and all that
it has lost by infidelity may be gained by fulfilling them. If, now, in place of a rational
probation of this kind, we suppose its opposite
to obtain, it is evident that we renounce all the
chief aids to salvation which man's moral nature
supplies. If we say that the law has been satis-
fied by an atonement, do we not render nugatory
the law, and blunt the point and invalidate the
force of the great Pauline announcement of
tribulation and anguish upon every soul whose
works are evil? If we declare that character is
estimated at its ethical worth up to a certain
period, say at death, or the " final judgment,"
and after that time moral distinctions are not
at all taken into account, but the soul's rank in

the scale of spiritual excellence is determined
by its having accepted or rejected that atonement, do we not juggle with righteousness and
weaken men's faith in the reality of the moral
order? Are we not in danger of confounding
moral distinctions and subverting ethics, if we
teach that a man who all his life has neglected
moral culture, has indeed been positively im-
moral, may be " saved " at the moment of death
by accepting the atonement and " casting himself on the merits of Christ"? Let us beware of
putting a premium on the last chance. Rather,
let us no longer teach that there is any last
chance. Our theology will be radically unsound
so long as this word " saved " is not emptied of
its magical meaning, is not " depolarized," — so
long, in fact, as it means anything to us but
abandonment of sin and growth into a moral
and spiritual life according to the psychological
laws of growth.

But not only is this theory of probation im-
moral, it may be questioned whether it does not
run counter to a right psychology. It rests
upon the presumption that immediately after
death, according to the old theology, or after
the " final judgment," according to the " new

theology," man enters upon an unchangeable
moral condition for eternity. Those who "die
in sin," according to one of these theologies,
those who are "finally impenitent," according
to the other, will be forever excluded from
righteousness. Right thinking and right living
are supposed to be in some way put out of their
reach. Now, in what way this is done or comes
about is a matter of great interest to psychology
and to ethics as well, as, indeed, is the question
whether or no it can happen at all. In the
first place there appears to lurk a contradiction
in the term "finally impenitent," affirmed of
beings having liberty of choice. Liberty and a
"final" condition are incompatible, since he
who can choose can never get himself into a
fixed or permanent state, even if he were to
choose to do so. The power of choice would
imply the power to get out of it. Final im-
penitence is an unpsychological fiction. But
the popular idea of the punishment of sin is
that it is brought about by the direct inter-
ference of the Deity ; and it would accord with
this idea to say that if man cannot get himself
into this fixed condition, then God can put him
into it. But in taking from man the power to

choose, that is, to change his moral condition, God would deprive him of that without which he would not be a human being. " Petrified into continuity of sinfulness," God's noblest creation would be discrowned and mutilated.[1] Some theologians put the close of the period of probation in an alleged permanency of character regarded as the natural consequence, under the laws of the soul, of long continuance in evil doing. A man, it is said, may become fixed in the habit of sinning, so that he cannot do otherwise than sin, — that is, cannot choose virtue. But he who cannot choose virtue cannot choose sin. To him who *can* do but one thing there is no choice; and where there is no choice there can be no sin, since sin is the choice of wrong when right might have been chosen. On this theory, then, a man may exercise and develop his power to sin to such a degree that he is no longer able to sin at all! The doctrine leads to an equal absurdity on the side of virtue. It involves a contradiction to say that a man may become.fixed in doing right in the sense that he cannot do wrong. For to do right in the ethi-

[1] The Doctrine of Probation Examined. By G. H. Emerson, D.D. Boston, 1883. p. 159.

cal sense implies a choice of right, and there is no choice of right to him who cannot choose wrong, since in a choice there must be two possibilities. He, then, who cannot do wrong is not a moral being, and cannot do right. Accordingly, the phrase "permanency of character" is a contradiction. A permanent character would be no character at all, since character involves freedom of choice.

IX. — UNIVERSALITY OF SALVATION.

Down to the present time in the history of the world salvation has been limited to a small number of men. Exactly what a disciple had in mind when he asked Jesus whether or no there be few that are saved, it may be difficult to determine. But the indirect answer of his Master is significant, "Strive to enter in at the narrow door." Did he mean by this answer that it is more important that each one strive to attain salvation than that he know how many do really attain it? But do the words, "Many shall seek to enter in and shall not be able," cut off hope for some? Rather the injunction to strive for admittance implies its possibility for all, and that the failure of some is due to

their defective seeking. That these will never
rightly seek and find an open door is by no
means implied. If by salvation we mean complete harmony with the universal moral and
spiritual order, then "the man Christ Jesus"
may well be the only one who has attained it.
But if "the narrow door" admit those who
knock at it, bearing, indeed, many defects, but
animated by a master-purpose to attain righteousness, then may many be regarded as having
entered in. But how vast has ever been and
is the number of those who do not care for
righteousness, and crowd the broad way so
pathetically pointed out by Jesus! That so
great a multitude of men wander in darkness
with "aimless feet," stumbling into degradation and bound in chains of passion, lust and
selfishness; that so many dark places on the
earth have not been visited with the healing
ministry of truth; that Nature holds relentless
sway, and smites with merciless retribution the
unhappy children of ignorance and sin; that
Cruelty scourges the weak and helpless till
Pity weeps and turns her face away; that Des-
potism grinds its subjects into the dust, and
smothers thought and manhood in Siberian

that the bitter ages are so long and
moral progress is so slow, — all these
reveal problems and mysteries at which
letters and reason is dumb. How far is
reign of the Kingdom of God
from its consummation! How do the tears and
agony of the Son of Man seem to have been in
vain, and the blood of martyrs to have been
poured out upon a thankless, fruitless earth!
Yet into the awful front of this mystery Faith
flings the great declaration that " God will have
all men to be saved and come to a knowledge of
the truth." Verily, of the times and the seasons
no man knoweth. This, however, we have
good reason to believe, that whatever may be
God's time, and in whatever mystery His
method may be hidden, He is the Universal
Father, and will, in His own way and season,
seek His lost, benighted children until He finds
them. If we are to believe in Jesus as an
interpreter of God's spirit and providence;
unless his ministry to men was a mask of love
and pity to hide the face of indifference and
mock the world with a show of sympathy; if
he truly represented the solicitude of Heaven for
men, — then must we believe that the Father's

heart is ever warm towards the prodigal, and the doors of His house stand ever open to the son who returns in penitence.

The universality of salvation — the hope of all and the faith of many — would be a most fitting consummation of a theistic government of the world, and is a very natural conclusion from its theistic origin. The salvation of a part and the ruin of the rest is a legitimate conclusion from Atheism. If the world, instead of being the product of Wisdom and Love, be the product of Chance, and have only a fortuitous development, the wonder were that not a part, but the whole, of the human race should not find its end in darkness. There are difficulties, no doubt, in interpreting the order of the world and of human life under the category of design. There are disorders and discords where we look for order and harmony, evil and weakness where we look for good and strength; the dark problem of heredity appears to indicate a design to propagate infirmity forever. But in spite of the difficulties which the world presents for a theistic theory, the alternative offered to thought is Theism and a beneficent purpose sometime to find its consummation in universal good, or Atheism with its corollary of infinite indefiniteness and uncertainty. The fact that we are unable to reconcile the existing physical and spiritual order with a beneficent purpose as we understand it, furnishes no presumption against the existence of such a purpose and its unbroken operation before our eyes. No one will dare maintain that the malign purpose of an unloving Creator is being fulfilled in the world and in man. The doctrines of the Fatherhood of God and the arbitrary, endless exclusion of any of His children from light and life furnish a contradiction which the human reason cannot endure. The love which " springs eternal in the human breast " would suffer endless unrest in view of the hard severity of a Father shutting the door of reconciliation against His penitent children. The saints in light, if they may be supposed to bear harps and crowns, would cast harp and crown at the foot of the throne, and declare themselves unworthy to worship the All-Holy, if it be not permitted them to speed to the world of pain with ministry of pity and message of peace and pardon. The doctrine which affirms the failure on the part of God to do all that He is able to do consistently with the nature of man to effect the salvation of all, denies His Fatherhood, and sets Him before men as a Being who cannot inspire trust, love, and worship in the highest meaning of these emotions. It is fatal to the noblest and purest expression of religion.

But if God fail not on His part, may not man fail and miss of salvation ? This dangerous gift of freedom, may it not prove the ruin of many ? Man is confronted with the conditions of salvation. If he do not accept them ? We have already seen that God cannot do violence to human freedom by limiting man's period of probation and preventing him from choosing salvation at any time in the existence of the soul, without destroying the integrity of the soul itself. He cannot, assuredly, do a similar violence in compelling man to accept the conditions of eternal life. Indeed, to accept must be voluntarily to take, freely to choose. Does the salvation of any or of all men, then, partake of the uncertainty which attaches to all forecast of results in which a free will is a factor ? From a purely speculative point of view, yes. Leaving God out of account, yes. But it is not alto-

gether a speculative question, and God may not
be left out of the account, will not be left out.
Indifferent and inactive, indeed, He cannot
be, — the God of Jesus and of the New Testament, the Father. Given this premise, and as
has already been pointed out, human reason cannot refuse the conclusion that the resources of
Divine wisdom, truth, and love will be employed
without reserve to win men from sin. Unhappily weak is the faith which admits the
doubt that these resources will be effectual in
compassing the utmost salvation. Will the Om-
nipotent, the All-loving, fail in such a task as
this ? Will truth be forever ineffectual against
error, light against darkness ? Will the Word
of God fail in teaching and enlightening the
darkened mind ? Will the obdurate, the hard-
hearted, resist endlessly the chastening of the
Divine love ? Are the remorse, the scourgings,
the darkness, which attend on disobedience
without terrors and motives for men ? Do not
the arid waste and desolation on which the
prodigal soul is stranded suggest the hospitable
plenty of the father's house, and bring the bewildered son to himself ? Shall the Son of Man,
who on earth went about doing good, have no

ministry of teaching, of healing and pity, wherever souls languish in sickness of sin? Will
his great prophecy fail of fulfilment, that if he
were lifted up from the earth he would draw
all men unto him?

Let us not disguise the difficulties which this
great problem of the salvation of all men has
presented and still presents to many, in view of
the power of sin in human nature; of the awful
record of depravity and degradation, of cruelty
and inhumanity; of the persistence of evil, rear-
ing its brazen, indomitable front through all the
ages of history; of the lapses of virtue and the
sudden fall of souls long steadfast from summits
of light into depths of darkness; of the appar-
ently ineffectual struggles and hopeless defeats
of the powers of good in their interminable conflict with the mighty forces of wrong; of the
slow progress and tardy triumphs of even the
good cause of the Christ, with its great original
Example and spiritual Light, and its vast army
of martyrs, scholars, heroes, and consecrated
leaders of pre-eminent genius and power. To
those whom this awful front and unconquered
presence of Wrong appall, who with faltering
confidence in right dare not affirm its ultimate

victory, there is no greater word to be spoken
than that of him who in his own person over-
came the world and proved the possibility of
victory for all: " Have faith in God." "It
sometimes puts a terrible strain upon our faith
in God's fatherhood to contemplate the sufferings of which this earth is so full ; to see the
millions of men who come into this world only
to be buffeted by its adversities and torn by its
severities, dragged through its hells and hurried
down to the dark death of the sinful. The only
thought which saves us from crying out of our
sympathizing hearts that God has made a fearful mistake in creating men is the faith, which
holds us in spite of all this misery, that God is
leading man through the shadows to the stars,
that strife and sorrow are growing less, and
man is being reclaimed and fitted for a true
sonship." [1]

Mr. John Stuart Mill, although inclined to
agnosticism, thought it conducive to mental and
moral health to believe in God and a future life,
if one could do so. Let the creed of optimism,
of the final prevalence of the moral and spiritual

[1] The Fatherhood of God (Manuals of Faith and Duty,
No. 1). By Rev. J. Coleman Adams, D.D. p. 88.

forces, be likewise commended to men. Happily it may be commended on abundant evidence. As the central thought and essential spirit of Christ; as a consummation without which his revelation of the Father is an enigma; as " the one far-off, divine event " towards which the development of man, as shown in history, appears to be surely moving ; as the only solution of the problem of evil, and the only satisfaction of the unrest of the " practical reason " of man in view of the struggles and hardships which virtue undergoes, — it has adequate support for a rational faith. It lies not far from the thought of the philosopher who interprets human life and history by the principle of evolution, nor from that of the poet to whom

" Through the ages one increasing purpose runs ; "

for he who through the ages of the world's history can trace a Divine purpose ever evoking order and good, is very near having attained the prophetic vision and faith by which such a purpose is seen to run victorious through the ages to come.

THE END.